NATIONAL FOOTBALL LEAGUE
SUPERSTARS 2007

★★★★★★★★★★★★★★

SCHOLASTIC INC.

New York   Toronto   London   Auckland   Sydney
Mexico City   New Delhi   Hong Kong   Buenos Aires

ISBN-13: 978-0-439-92454-2
ISBN-10: 0-439-92454-5

Published by Scholastic Inc.
SCHOLASTIC and associated logos are trademarks and/or registered trademarks of Scholastic Inc.

12 11 10 9 8 7 6 5 4 3 2   7 8 9 10 11/0

Printed in the U.S.A.
First printing, August 2007

Ronde Barber

The race isn't always won by the person who runs the fastest, jumps the highest, or pushes the hardest. Many times the race is won by the competitor who makes the most of his abilities, the one who wants to win more than anyone.

And this is why Ronde Barber has been one of the best cornerbacks in the NFL for the last ten seasons.

For sure, Ronde possesses enormous athletic skills. In addition to football, he participated in track and wrestling at Cave Spring High School in Roanoke, Virginia. At the same time, the 5-foot-10, 184-pounder doesn't have what is considered to be the ideal size and speed to stay in step with the taller, faster wide receivers in the league. No matter. Ronde was selected to play in three of the last five Pro Bowl games. In addition, he is the first and only cornerback to record at least 20 sacks and 20 interceptions in his career.

Ronde (which is short for Orondé, his middle name) is the identical twin of Tiki Barber, the New York Giants halfback. While Tiki gets more headlines and television time — after all, he handles the ball more often and scores more touchdowns — Ronde has something that his brother doesn't have and wants very badly.

It's called a Super Bowl ring.

Ronde got his in the 2002 season, when he made the most important play of his career. In the fourth quarter of the NFC Championship game in Philadelphia, he intercepted a pass and returned it 92 yards for a touchdown to clinch the 27–10 victory.

It was another race that Ronde won even though he wasn't the biggest or the fastest or the strongest player on the field.

Tom Brady

You never know when the opportunity for success will come your way. But when the moment comes, you can either grab it and take it a long way or fumble it and go nowhere.

Take New England Patriots quarterback Tom Brady, for instance.

Tom started his second season on the bench. Suddenly, on September 23, 2001, his life changed with one play. Patriots starter Drew Bledsoe went down with a serious injury, and just like that, Tom was called on to take over the team. It took awhile for Tom to get settled, but once he was, he led the Patriots to the championship and was named Super Bowl XXXVI Most Valuable Player.

Two years later, the Patriots won another Super Bowl, and Tom won another MVP award. One year after that, they won the Super Bowl yet again, their third in a span of four years. Along the way, the Brady bunch won 21 consecutive games, a league record.

"I'm only as good as they are, and they're only as good as I am," Tom says. "So we're in this together, myself and the receivers."

Not everybody thought the kid from San Mateo, California, would ever be this successful, though.

At the University of Michigan, Tom sat on the bench for his first two years. Even though he led his team to an Orange Bowl victory in his final game there, many scouts believed Tom wasn't strong enough to excel at the next level. In the NFL draft a few months later, 198 players were chosen ahead of him.

Now many people compare Tom with former San Francisco 49ers quarterback Joe Montana, whom Tom often watched as a kid. Not only has he grabbed the moment, but it looks as if Tom, like his idol, will run with it all the way to the Hall of Fame.

Reggie Bush

New Orleans Saints scatback Reggie Bush has many nicknames. One is The President, because he and George W. Bush share the same last name. Teammate Joe Horn refers to Reggie as Baby Matrix. Like the characters in *The Matrix* movies, he seems to move faster than is humanly possible.

In Louisiana, Reggie is known as Saint Reggie because of the way he lifted the playoff hopes of a team and the spirits of a city.

"I'm not trying to be savior," says the 21-year-old kid who calls himself plain ol' Reggie. "I'm just trying to help win some games and maybe a Super Bowl someday."

No athlete or sports team will rebuild New Orleans after the tragedy of Hurricane Katrina, but at a time when the city needed some hope for the future and distraction from the present, Reggie provided it by carrying a football. And he carried it fast, very, very fast.

After his final year at the University of Southern California, where he was also an excellent student, Reggie was expected to be the number-one pick in the NFL draft. In one workout, he ran the 40-yard dash in 4.33 seconds, had a standing broad jump of 10-foot-9, a vertical leap of 40.5 inches, and did 24 repetitions in the 225-pound bench press! But the Houston Texans surprised almost everybody by choosing a different player. Some consider it a miracle that Reggie was left for the Saints, who were quick to make him the second selection.

New Orleans residents were so giddy about the news that, in a matter of days, hundreds of them had already bought his jersey. Reggie was just as excited to be one of them, quickly becoming part of the community. He donated some of the money from the jersey sales to hurricane victims, and paid to fix a high school football field and save a school.

And while the Saints fell short of a spot in Super Bowl LXVI there was a lot to celebrate. Saint Reggie may not really be a saint, but he is a gift to New Orleans.

Rudi Johnson

The life of a professional athlete isn't always fun and games. As Cincinnati Bengals star runner Rudi Johnson can tell you, it's also about patience and desire and sometimes even pain.

At the time Rudi was chosen in the fourth round of the 2001 NFL draft, the Bengals weren't a very good team. Even so, Rudi spent more time on the bench than he did on the field. It wasn't until his third season that the former Auburn University star got his chance to play on a regular basis.

When his number was finally called, Rudi made the most of the opportunity. In 2005, he gained a team record 1,458 yards and scored 12 touchdowns. The Bengals workhorse touched the ball 360 times and fumbled only once!

Even more remarkable, Rudi had his best season despite the torn cartilage in his left knee. The injury was especially difficult for Rudi, a 5-foot-10, 220-pound fireplug, who relied on the strength of his legs to generate power. It took him an extra twenty-five minutes to loosen up before each game.

After knee surgery, Rudi spent a lot of time improving his physical condition. He even went on a special diet.

"I understand how hard you have to work and how hard you have to play," says Rudi, who is even quicker and faster now. "And I understand you have to do it all the time, every single week, and not just some of the time."

If Rudi was so good while he played in pain, how much better will he be now? The rest of the league probably doesn't want to know the answer.

Walter Jones

What's the safest, surest road in Seattle these days? Try Route 71. That's the jersey number of Seahawks tackle Walter Jones, the human road-grater who clears the widest, smoothest path of any offensive lineman in professional football.

At 6 foot 5, Walter is big enough to blot out the sun. At 315 pounds, he's strong enough to move small mountains. Yet athletes that large and that muscular aren't supposed to move as well as Walter does. The former Florida State University star is so unusually light on his feet that he has been known to make plays as far as 20 yards downfield.

Last season Walter was on the road to the Super Bowl, where the Seahawks went for the first time in their history. Walter protected Matt Hasselbeck so well that the quarterback calls him "probably the best player in the league." Star halfback Shaun Alexander scored the majority of his NFL record 28 touchdowns on the left side, where Walter lined up almost every play.

In fact, Walter was so good that the coaches gave him the highest possible grade in 17 of 19 games! Then again, as Walter says, "We set our standards very high."

Usually, the names of offensive linemen become known only when they miss blocks or commit penalties. Not Walter's, though. After his six Pro Bowl appearances, everyone from East coast to West is well aware of who he is — the express lane of the Seahawks offense.

Matt Leinart

Almost everything about Matt Leinart seems right. The Arizona Cardinals quarterback throws accurate spirals, and not only did he win the Heisman Trophy as the best player in college football, but he led the University of Southern California to a 13–0 record and the national championship in the 2004 season.

Yet life hasn't always been perfect for Mr. Perfect. Far from it, in fact.

You see, Matt was born with crossed eyes — the left one was not aligned properly with the right — a condition known as strabismus. At 3 years old, he underwent surgery and was fitted with special glasses to correct the problem. To make matters worse, in grammar school, Matt was overweight. Because of the odd glasses and the extra pounds, he was often teased and taunted by classmates.

"I used to get made fun of for being cross-eyed," Matt remembers. "It's just a terrible thing, because kids are so cruel to the fat

kid, to the kid with the glasses. So I turned to sports."

At Mater Dei High School in California, it didn't take long for Matt to show he was a natural. Moving on to college at USC, Matt was so cool, so smart, so talented that he could have been the number-one pick in the 2005 NFL draft in his junior year.

At that point, Matt had a difficult decision to make. Would he return to USC for one final year, or would he turn pro?

After much thought, Matt stayed put. He didn't regret it, either. While Matt enjoyed one last year of college life with his friends, he guided the Trojans to a 12–1 record. The Cardinals drafted the left-hander in the first round weeks later, and he quickly became one of the best young quarterbacks in the league.

Funny, isn't it, that some of those who once made fun of the chubby kid with the strange glasses are probably cheering for him now?

Peyton Manning

Little brothers and big brothers often have close relationships. So when the two have to compete against each other, it can be a sticky situation, to say the least.

Now imagine how Indianapolis Colts golden arm Peyton Manning felt when he had to play his younger brother, Eli, of the New York Giants in the first game of the 2006 season. (At thirty, Peyton is five years older than Eli.) It was the first time in NFL history that two brothers had started at quarterback in the same game.

As it turned out, Peyton did what most big brothers would do — he taught his little brother a lesson, then patted him on the back and wished him luck when the game was over.

Both the Manning brothers played well, but Peyton got the best of Eli where it counted most — on the scoreboard. The Colts won with a 26–21 score.

"It's pretty awesome when you think about it," said Peyton. "If it happens again, I want to meet the two brothers."

Eli shouldn't be too upset about what happened, though, because his big brother beat a lot of teams over the years. In the 2005 season, for example, Peyton led the Colts to 13 consecutive victories before they lost for the first time.

Known for his smarts and strong, accurate arm, Peyton holds several NFL records. The list includes most touchdown passes in a season (49) as well as consecutive seasons with more than 4,000 yards in the air (6).

On February 4, 2007, Peyton earned a place on the ultimate list: Super Bowl Champions. He led the Colts to a 29-17 victory over the Chicago Bears. In spite of the rain, Peyton was in complete control of the game, earning the Most Valuable Player award and adding to his legend.

Then again, Peyton had a pretty good teacher himself. His and Eli's father is Archie Manning, once a New Orleans Saints quarterback.

Clinton Portis

Professional football can be very serious business. So Clinton Portis decided to liven things up on practice days early in the 2005 season.

In interviews with reporters, the Washington Redskins halfback wore the costumes of several characters that he had invented. There was Coach Janky Spanky. Also Coconut Jones. And Dolla Bill. And Dr. I Don't Know. Inspector 2–2. Rev. Gonna Change. Sheriff Gonna Getcha. Sir Lend-me-a-hand. Southeast Jerome. The Mad Scientist.

Clinton even included their pictures in his Christmas cards.

"It's about coming together," Clinton explains. "Everyone around here is having fun. There's nobody who can be uptight when they see me like this."

But when Clinton dresses up in a gold and burgundy jersey on game days, he can make opponents a bit nervous. In 2005, he ran over and around them for a team record 1,516 yards and scored 12 touchdowns.

Clinton had led the undefeated University of Miami to the 2001 national championship, then the Denver Broncos picked him in the second round of the NFL draft one year later. After two excellent seasons with the Broncos, Clinton was traded to the Redskins. To get Portis from the Broncos, the Redskins gave up their own big name player, cornerback Champ Bailey. The trade became one of the most talked about in league history as people debated whether it was easier to replace a running back or a cornerback. Clinton would quickly demonstrate that the Redskins had made a good choice with this deal.

Since then, not even a partially dislocated shoulder, which Clinton suffered in a preseason game in the summer of 2005, has been able to stop him. A few weeks after the injury, he was all dressed up and ready to start the 2006 regular season.

That's No-Quittin' Clinton, the character that Redskins fans have come to know and love most of all.

Tony Romo

To play quarterback for the Dallas Cowboys is one of the greatest dream jobs in all of sports. From Roger Staubach, who guided the Cowboys to a pair of Super Bowl victories, to Troy Aikman, who led them to three more, some of the most famous names in football have played the position in Dallas.

So how did this Tony Romo guy get into the club?

You see, the typical Cowboys quarterback is a big name who has done big things at a big college before he has turned pro. Tony did some big things in college, all right, but he did them at Eastern Illinois University, which had a small football program in the tiny town of Charleston, Illinois. So while Tony received the Walter Payton Award as the best player at the Division I-AA level in the 2002 season, his name wasn't seen in many headlines around the country. Sure enough, every NFL team passed over him in the draft.

A few months later, the Cowboys signed Tony as their third-string quarterback. It took a lot of hard work and patience — and a little bit of luck — but midway through the 2006 season, he finally got his chance to start an NFL game. And another. And another. And Tony and his strong arm and quick feet didn't stop until they reached the playoffs.

In fact, Tony was so good that he was selected to the Pro Bowl team even though he started only nine games!

The dream season finally ended on a rainy night in Seattle, where Tony fumbled a slippery ball on a field-goal attempt in the final seconds. "I take responsibility for messing up at the end there," the QB said while he fought back tears. "That's my fault, and I cost the Dallas Cowboys a playoff win."

Yet while Tony took the loss hard, it couldn't ruin one of the feel-good stories of the football season. After all, who would have thought the unknown kid from the small school in the small town would eventually become the big man in Big D?

Michael Strahan

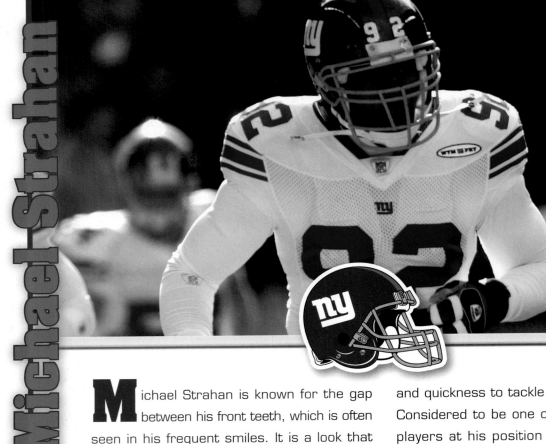

Michael Strahan is known for the gap between his front teeth, which is often seen in his frequent smiles. It is a look that rival quarterbacks have become very familiar with over the years. After all, Michael has sacked 60 different ones in his 14-season career!

The primary purpose of a defensive end is to pressure the quarterback, a role that is one of the most important on the field in an age of pass-happy offenses. And few, if any, players have done it better than Michael, who at 6 foot 5 and 275 pounds is a true giant among New York Giants.

Michael entered the 2006 season with 129.5 sacks in his career, the ninth-highest total in NFL history. His 22.5 sacks in 2001 stand as the league record for one season. (Sacks first became an official statistic in the 1982 season.)

Yet what makes Michael so unique is that, not only does he put pressure on quarterbacks, but he has the smarts, strength, and quickness to tackle ball carriers as well. Considered to be one of the best all-around players at his position in quite some time, Michael was selected to play in seven of the last nine Pro Bowl games.

Born in Houston, Texas, Michael had a somewhat late start in the sport. He played football only one year in high school before he moved to Germany, where his father was stationed in the United States Army. When Michael returned home, he attended Texas Southern University and was selected in the second round of the 1993 draft.

Michael will turn thirty-five years old this season, but when sports fans see him still wreaking havoc on the field after all these years, they'll know that quarterbacks haven't seen the last of his smile for a while.

LaDainian Tomlinson

Who is the best all-around runner in professional football? It is the question that is asked as frequently as any other each season. Unless someone has been trapped inside a very dark cave lately, the name of San Diego Chargers superstar runner LaDainian Tomlinson is sure to be one of the first to roll off their tongue. In fact, L.T. recieved the NFL Most Valuable Player Award for 2006.

A rare 5-foot-11, 221-pound package of speed, power, and grit, LaDainian has established himself as one of the NFL greats in only five seasons. In December, L.T. scored his 29th touchdown of the season, a new league record.

"I believe LaDainian is the finest running back to ever wear an NFL uniform," says Chargers head coach Marty Schottenheimer, who has seen many of them over the years.

At 27 years of age, LaDainian isn't done yet. If he stays healthy, L.T. may challenge retired Dallas Cowboys great Emmitt Smith as the number-one ground-gainer in league history. Emmitt also happens to be his boyhood idol.

Yet what separates LaDaininan from many of the other great backs is his ability to catch the football and even throw it sometimes. In fact, he passed for three touchdowns last year! Before this season, L.T. scored 72 times as a runner, eight as a receiver and four as a passer.

"I'm in great shape," says LaDainian, a Texas Christian University graduate. "This is what I do."

Just as LaDainian is more than a one-trick pony on the field, he has many interests off it as well. In his spare time, L.T. likes to travel, watch movies, play golf and basketball, and help kids in the San Diego area. He also is into classic cars and has a cherry-red 1964 Chevy Impala in his collection.

LaDainian has a motor that just won't quit, and one day soon it will carry him to the Super Bowl.

Brian Urlacher

Chicago Bears star linebacker Brian Urlacher was born in Pasco, Washington, and, after his parents divorced, grew up in Lovington, New Mexico.

And, boy, did Brian ever grow up!

Before he graduated from Lovington High School, Brian shot up nearly five inches, gained more than 60 pounds, and led the football team to an undefeated season. In fact, Brian was so fast and powerful that he played both ways — wide receiver on offense, and safety on defense.

Brian wanted to attend Texas Tech University, but he was not offered a scholarship there. Finally, he chose the University of New Mexico. It wasn't until Brian was used as a safety wide receiver and kick returner that the NFL scouts began to notice his athletic talents.

The Bears chose Brian in the first round of the 2000 draft. In his first season, Brian was selected Rookie of the Year and was asked to play in the Pro Bowl game. It wasn't long before his No. 54 jersey became one of the most popular in the country.

For Brian, the 2005 season was his best yet. Known for his ability to make plays all over the field, Brian was named Defensive Player of the Year and received another Pro Bowl invitation.

"All that stuff is great, good, whoop-de-doo," Brian says of his individual accomplishments. "But I want a Super Bowl ring."

When Brian doesn't play football, he likes to travel, play Ping-Pong, drink chocolate milk, and help others. He once won $47,000 on the *Wheel of Fortune* game show and donated the money to charity! He also spends many hours assisting the Special Olympics and other charities. And he's never too busy to sign autographs.

As Brian proves, it's possible to be a rough, tough Chicago Bear on the field and a big ol' teddy bear off it.

Hines Ward

Like the city they represent, the Pittsburgh Steelers are a close-knit team, the kind that isn't afraid to get down and dirty if it means a job well done.

If ever there was a person made to be a Steeler, then Hines Ward is it.

One of the few professional athletes playing in the U.S. to be born in South Korea, Hines isn't your typical star wide receiver. The best players in this position almost always run the fastest, move the quickest, and jump the highest. While Hines can do those things well — he has caught more passes than anyone in Steelers history — he plays a more physical game. He prefers to run over opponents rather than around them.

Wide receivers aren't known for their ability to block, but Hines likes to lead the way for his teammates. In fact, many experts say that nobody in the league does it better than Hines. That helps explain why every season the Steelers run the ball better than most other teams do.

The hard work paid off for the Steelers in Super Bowl XL, and Hines played an XL-size role in the 21–10 victory. He caught five passes and scored one touchdown, a 43-yarder that sealed the deal in the fourth quarter. He was named the Most Valuable Player of the game.

Rather than talk about his own performance afterward, Hines focused on what the Steelers had done as a team. After all, there may be an i in Pittsburgh, but as Hines will tell you, it's the u and s that count most.

Brian Westbrook

Have you ever been overshadowed by the most popular or talented person in school? Have you ever wondered what would happen if it was your time to shine?

Well, you're not alone, because Philadelphia Eagles halfback Brian Westbrook used to wonder the very same thing.

In his first four seasons in the NFL, he played in the shadow of Donovan McNabb, his Eagles teammate. Oh, it wasn't like the 5-foot-8, 200-pound package of flash and dash was unknown. It was just that Donovan was the quarterback, and one of the most visible and valuable players in the league.

In mid-November of the 2006 season, however, all of that changed. Donovan went down with an injury that forced him to sit out the rest of the season.

With their quarterback out of action, all of a sudden, Brian was The Man. To the surprise of many people, the Eagles bounced back from what could have been a season ending moment and won. Then they won some more. They didn't stop winning until they'd captured the division title and Brian had gained 1,217 yards, the most of his career.

"Big-time players step up when you need them the most," Brian explains.

In high school, the then 5-foot-2, Brian attended college at Villanova. In the 2001 season, he was selected for the Walter Payton Award as the best college player, but because Brian had played at the Division I-AA level, he was overlooked in the first two rounds of the NFL draft. Finally, the Eagles drafted him in the third round, partly because Villanova was located in Philadelphia and they were familiar with him.

Since then, Brian has been one of the best all-around backs in the league. He catches passes. He returns punts. He carries the ball inside. He carries the ball outside. And now we know he can carry a team, too.

Vince Young

When everything is fine, it's easy for a person to act like he doesn't have a care in the world. But it's how he responds under pressure that says a lot more about him.

Of course, it helps when you're usually the quickest, fastest athlete on the field. "What I try to do is keep defenses on edge, not knowing if I'm going to run or pass," Vince explains. "I always go out there trying to be their worst nightmare."

In the 2006 Rose Bowl game, Vince and the Texas Longhorns became the University of Southern California's worst nightmare. USC was undefeated that season and had won 34 games in a row. No matter. The Longhorns were undefeated too, and they had a secret weapon: Vince Young. With 19 seconds on the clock, Vince ran past the Trojans for a touchdown that clinched a 41–38 victory. Texas won the National Championship — its first in 35 years — and Vince was elevated to legendary status.

After Vince set all kinds of records in college — in his final year, he became the only player to pass for 3,000 yards and run for 1,000 yards in the same season — the Titans selected him in the first round of the NFL draft. Like most rookies, he had to watch, listen, and learn on the sidelines for a while. But when Vince got his chance midway through the season, he acted like he had been in the pros for years.

Just ask the Manning brothers.

In November 2006, Vince led the Titans past Eli Manning and the New York Giants. The next week he upset Peyton Manning and the Indianapolis Colts. Performances like this helped earn Vince the AP Offensive Rookie of the Year Award. Not bad for a first season.

Then again, Vince learned what it took to beat an even tougher opponent a long time ago. Vince was 6 years old and riding his bicycle on a Houston street when he was struck by a van. The handle bar of the bike stuck in his stomach, and he ended up in the hospital for several months. The experience changed his life and made him a stronger person.

Now if we could only see him sweat for once . . .